Journey of My Life

By Sabrina Blocker

Copyright

Copyright © 2020 by Sabrina Blocker

Printed in the United States of America

First Printing, 2020

ISBN 9798688541892

Editor: Dominique Lambright @ dmleditingandwriting.com
Book Coach: Erica Blocker @ https://ericablocker.com

Table of Contents

Sabrina Blocker

Dedication

I dedicate this book to my sons, Yusef and Nasir. Never let anyone or anything stop you from living your life. Follow God and follow your dreams.

Love,

Mom

Sabrina Blocker

Gratitude

I want to say a special thank you to Alisa Blocker
Williams, Erica Blocker, and Vinsetta Tyann
Robertson – my riders.

Introduction

My transparency is for a cause. Hopefully, it will help you feel better, do better, and be encouraged.

My prayer is that this book of poems will empower you to live and not die. I pray that it helps you to keep pressing in the middle of life's storms. I have been through abandonment, heartbreak, heartache, mental, physical, and verbal abuse, divorce, depression, anxiety, and fear. I can honestly say that I broke free from the pain of my past by trusting God to make a way and by doing the work to overcome my issues. Some of the work I did included journaling, praying, and reading literature that discusses the issues I had. Most of all, I kept the faith that God would bring me through all of it.

After the darkest days, things DO get brighter and better.

Love,

Sabrina

"I am not her who I used to be. I am now she, who God has created me to be."

Sabrina Blocker

Girl Power - How We Roll

We come back from the dead strong. Unbreakable even when lied on, punched on, even being deceived. All kinds of things have been done to our breed.

Deserving the best but sometimes getting the worst.

Can walk armed with nothing in our purse—low food, no clothes most of the time, not a dime.

But pack out the churches and looking fine.

Knowing God is our help and always our strength.

We fight hard through the struggle, no matter the length.

Hard lives, hard times, and little or no direction.

God's mighty hand being our protection.

Since the beginning of time, we've been cursed with pain, enduring more obstacles than anyone but God could understand but not giving up because God has a plan.

Powerful but still gentle.

We're born with a soft touch and still know how to survive when not given much.

Run a whole household, raise our kids alone,
knowing King Jesus is right there on the throne.

Deserve to be respected, loved, and adored.

Leaning on Jesus, our strength He restores.

Will always be a lady, even those lost and working
the poles.

We have a hard job, most searching to be whole.

Never gonna give up, gonna stay strong 'til our end.

And when treated right, will be your best friend.

Creepin'

Didn't you know he was mine?

Sure, you did. That's why you only spoke to him at certain times.

Knew all about the kids and me.

Where else did you think he lived?

Creep, creep every day of the week.

You'll never have a good man in him; that's why his vows to me he didn't keep.

He lied to me. He's gonna lie to you.

He cheated on me; it will be the same for you.

He never kept a job, but you think he's gonna "diamond" you.

The heartbreak I felt will soon be you, too.

Overcomers

Look how we're made.

Built to perfection.

Handcrafted by God, beautiful and strong.

Made to endure since the beginning like Eve.

We are necessary, not just to man, but to the world.

Women with purpose, we are God's intentional creation.

We birth a nation.

We are made overcomers.

Mothers, sisters, friends, she, her feminine, lawyers, pastors, doctors, engineers, and anything a man can do.

Live out your dreams, no matter what you face in life.

No matter how hard the journey of life.

Trust God.

Our lives have a destiny to reach.

Keep living, praying, believing, and overcoming, for that is how we're made.

Be strong, be bold, be better, be blessed!

Purpose

My pain will push me to my purpose so that I can be all that I was intended to be.

The issues of life and all that happened will make me stronger.

Sharing my story, which is not unique, will enable the next woman to push.

Push past the fear, bad memories, low self-esteem, and become who you are intended to be.

Don't let the truth be too hard to deal with, but let it be a guide into the future.

Embrace the past and use it to push yourself forward.

Everything that stops gives opportunity for a new start.

Used

I was your opportunity. You never loved me. Just wanted to try to destroy the life you saw in me.

Used me to raise the kids you had, the same ones you always left me with when you ran the streets.

How could you be like that? Such a sorry and horrible man. No parts of good – just busted.

You intended to use me. That's why you always begged and lied to return to me.

Now you're not gonna be a part of my destiny.

You're no good for me and never were.

I deserve so much better.

You're gonna miss the best you ever had.

You're gonna get just what you deserve.

God made me special, and my soul, you can't have – no matter how hard you tried to break me.

You didn't succeed in your plan.

He Knows

God knows what's best for me.

That's why he pulled me out of the mess.

It was sucking the breath right out of me.

God knew when it was time for a change.

He knew that my life He would rearrange.

Saved me from myself, which was weak.

Showed me the promises He said He would keep.

God has my back, my front, and keeps me on both sides.

In His arms, there is shelter where I can run and hide.

Opened my eyes and put praise in my heart.

He has always been there from the very start.

Thank you, God, for knowing what's best and letting me recover from the set up that tried to destroy me.

I will praise you forever 'cause you are my king.

In you, I now have victory.

Thanks, Jesus

Lifter of my head

Thanks, Jesus.

Helping with this pain

Thanks, Jesus.

Paying all these bills.

Thanks, Jesus.

Helping me raise my kids.

Thanks, Jesus.

Sleeping with me every night.

Thanks, Jesus.

Being a friend when I'm lonely.

Thanks, Jesus.

Knowing everything I go through.

Thanks, Jesus.

Putting a smile where there's a cry.

Thanks, Jesus.

Walking with me every day and every second.

Sabrina Blocker

Thanks, Jesus.

You Shall Live

You shall live and not die.

That's what God said to me.

I felt it inside.

Dry all your tears, cry if you need.

I have you, girl. You are my seed.

I'm not gonna let you go.

I am right here, continue to live your life, and have
no fear.

I know you're hurting and feel so much pain, but
you're gonna live.

It's just that plain.

Sabrina Blocker

New Life

New life you've given me.

A chance for something different.

To show me your love, not the abuse that was given to me.

To lift me up, not put me down.

Wanting me to continue to grow.

You created this smile and a heart as warm as fire.

My gentle love is what you want me to continue to give.

I'm a product of your strength.

Your strength moves me.

Learning, being a light, and always reppin' Jesus.

Moving me past my past.

Leaving the old people and things behind.

New Hope, New Future, New Mercies, New Me.

My Blessings

Blessings from God, I never thought I could have.

Both of you, to my literal surprise.

Outside of God through Jesus, you show me, pure love.

Both so different but equally wonderful.

The best gift besides Jesus that God ever gave me.

I'm so thankful to have both of you; my world has become a happier place.

I know that God knew I needed you as much as you need me.

Being your mom gives me purpose, balance, joy, smiles, laughter, and company.

I'm so grateful, thankful, and proud of you – Yusef and Nasir.

You'll never have to look for me 'cause I'll always be near.

Even when I go to be with Jesus, I'll still live in you.

I'll be smiling from heaven waiting because we'll be together again.

Thank you, God, for my blessings, my sons you
gave to me.

Days Like Today

Days like today, when it rains and the sun is not shining bright, I have to seek your face that much harder.

I know your presence is still there, but I seem to feel a little more down – maybe because sometimes I feel that no one is around.

I pray all day 'cause my mind drifts back to the pain of yesterday.

I'm holding on to you, oh Lord, and holding on to your word that you'll never leave me.

I have to trust that you're here sitting with me now.

Playing Games

Why do you still call me if you don't love me?

What makes you bother to pick up the phone?

If you wanted to be with her so bad, why isn't she
your all in all?

I have a hard enough time trying to forget you and
all the years and memories we shared.

This bittersweet thing that's going on between us
has got to end.

You're still the same person I knew.

Nothing about you has changed.

It's like you want to keep hurting me every time
you call.

If you're not ever-changing or sending me a dime,
you should just stop calling and wasting my time.

Finally Free

The absence of pain. The feeling of joy.

Oh, to ride this wave is like nothing I ever felt before.

Totally lifted. Could care less.

Feels so good inside—joy from Jesus.

He visited me. Again and again, it's lovely.

Released, relieved, and feel so pure.

Whole never before, but whole now.

Nothing broken. My heart is fixed.

My mind is made up to be walking in Victory.

Didn't come easy.

I fought really hard, hurt really bad, but God knew 'cause He knows everything, and He knows me.

I'm His child.

Took some time, but I know it was Him.

Nobody could remove the pain of the cup size that I carried but Him.

To have my breakthrough. To cry it all out. To have it removed and to smile again is beautiful.

I have peace.

Finally, I'm free.

I'm riding on His clouds not because my life is perfect, but because God is perfect.

His love for me is amazing.

Hold On

If you hold on, it will get better.

Every burden, every struggle gets lighter and lighter
day by day if you hold out and don't stress.

Give your troubles over to God, then press your
way through each day.

If you don't focus too much on the trouble, you'll
be busy on the better.

Never spend too much time on your problems –
they get too large.

Make God larger than your problems, and you will
see the load unload.

Change the things you can change.

The things you can't change, you still can't change.

Why suffer and stress over life or circumstances,
wasting time and energy?

We were given this life to live with love, peace, and
enjoyment.

Yes, pain and struggle are real, but so is casting
your cares on the Lord.

He cares for you.

If you believe and follow Him, He will see you through.

Trust, believe, and watch the miracles and wonders He can perform.

Direction

Feel fear, just do it.

No joy, there's hope.

Feel pain; it will go away.

When it returns, just pray.

No direction, call out to your guide.

Feel lost, let God live inside.

Feel pressure, release in prayer.

Feel hopeless; let faith be a guide for your future.

Believe you can.

Know that there is a promise that God will never leave when others will.

Dream and live.

Keep pushing.

Feel better, and keep trying.

Sabrina Blocker

Every Day

Every day is a blessing.

Every day is a new beginning.

Every day is a gift from God

Every day is special

Every day is to be enjoyed.

Exercise faith every day.

Love God every day.

Love myself every day.

Love Is

Love is believing in change.

It is hope. It is forgiving.

Love is trust in God because He is bigger than us.
Bigger than the problem.

Love is making things new

It is talking and laughing.

Love is staying when you want to quit

Love is trying over and over again.

Love is forever.

Sabrina Blocker

You've Been There

I look back over my life, you've been there.

Through hard times and dark times, you've been there.

In good times where there were smiles, you've been there.

Times spent with people who didn't care, you've been there.

While my life has had many struggles, you've been there.

When I felt lost and afraid, you've been there.

When life beat me down to the ground, you've been there.

When I became a mother to my sons, you've been there.

Raised children who turned on me and weren't even mine, you've been there.

When my ex-husband treated me like dirt, you've been there.

When I needed someone to love me, you've been there.

When I needed to be saved from myself, you've been there.

When I die and look for Jesus, I pray you're still right there.

Love Again

I remember love.

To feel good, smiling, and love songs.

It's okay to be open after the hurt.

It's safe to love again.

The great energy.

To feel warm, safe, free, and sexy.

The look of someone loving you, wanting you, and ready to explore.

Let go, let it go, the past pain, the bondage of a bad place.

Open up to the freedom of something new.

Love songs, slow dancing, a warm embrace.

Not wanting the night to end.

Watching the sun come up while waiting for the next phone call.

That's real.

The blush, the "I love you," "I want you," "I never want to leave you."

My world, my girl, my wife, my life, my love, my friend, my gem.

That's love.

It feels so good.

Remembering love and readying for a new one.